AUGUSTINE

IN

CARTHAGE

And Other Poems

AUGUSTINE
IN
CARTHAGE

And Other Poems

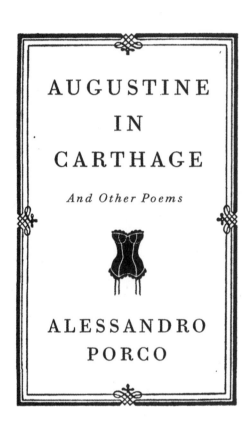

ALESSANDRO
PORCO

ECW

Published by ECW Press, 2120 Queen Street East, Suite 200,
Toronto, Ontario, Canada M4E 1E2

LIBRARY AND ARCHIVES CANADA CATALOGUING IN PUBLICATION

Porco, Alessandro
Augustine in Carthage and other poems / Alessandro Porco.

"a misFit book."
ISBN 978-1-55022-818-2

I. Title.

PS8631.O73A84 2008   c811'.6   c2007-907105-8

Editor for the press: Michael Holmes / a misFit book
Type: Rachel Brooks
Cover Design: David Gee
Printing: Coach House Printing

The publication of *Augustine in Carthage* has been generously supported by the Canada
Council for the Arts, which last year invested $20.1 million in writing and publishing
throughout Canada, by the Ontario Arts Council, by the Government of Ontario through
Ontario Book Publishing Tax Credit, by the OMDC Book Fund, an initiative of the
Ontario Media Development Corporation, and by the Government of Canada
through the Book Publishing Industry Development Program (BPIDP).

Canada Council   Conseil des Arts   Canada   ONTARIO ARTS COUNCIL
for the Arts   du Canada   CONSEIL DES ARTS DE L'ONTARIO

DISTRIBUTION
CANADA: Jaguar Book Group, 100 Armstrong Ave., Georgetown, ON, L7G 5S4

PRINTED AND BOUND IN CANADA

MISFIT

ECW PRESS
ecwpress.com

There is a bit of testicle at the bottom of our most sublime feelings and our purest tenderness.

— Diderot

to Brenna

Contents

Augustine in Carthage

I said to my soul, be still, and wait without hope.
                                                    — T.S. Eliot

I came upon the shore and, from the sand,
with one step forward, found myself in *Club
Super Sexe*, where Manon-from-Dorion's
torsion around the pole was more mannered
than the *figura serpentinata*
of Bologna's *The Rape of the Sabine*;
where a daisy Daisy-from-Dégelis made me dizzy,
performing swivel-roll upon -roll, with an acrobat's
grace, across the acrylic stage, despite
her sacrum, swollen like my nutsack, *tabarnak*;
and with Joliette-from-Lachine, my head
happily vised between her chi-chis, I thought,
"It was you, Joliette, it was you, who
inspired Clément Marot's blazon 'Le Beau Tétin'";
and a caryatid Lucky hoisting Luscious,
she (Lucky) lapped at Luscious's lucky labium
with the plastered feverishness of a cold-
blooded fish; and, Berri, a half-Cree
from Baie-James, gyrating her country hips
atop my stoic dick, spoke into my ear, *sotto voce*,
"Whatever is going to happen is already."
Every ecdysiast's twat was bald,
and I do recall criminal fuzz of Souk Ahras pubes
catching more skuzz than a copper's blotter.
I downed my watered-down draft, and with a
polite tip, and tip of my Kangol, in thanks,
to the doorman, I exited to "Le Grand Saint Cat" —

"Liberties of London," since 1978,
sandwiched between a deli and a *babyGap*,
official sponsor of *Club Super Sexe*,
"providing undersized apparel since 1982."
Streetside, *Club Petronius*'s proteinaceous crowd
of feasters swallowed the street they spit into
like Seamen during Fleet Week: a thousand Gitons's
nipples nibbled, testicles tickled, perineums rubbed,
fingertips as sweet-scented as pomanders,
according to Sandy Salivas wettin' their lips.
Pushing through I was bum-rushed by a bum;
like a cub, having just narrowly escaped
the bear-baiting ring, is how I would describe
his confused state. He sang this little ditty:
"I lost my cock to the war on terror,
I kept peace in the sheets of an Afghan whore;
two months ago I completed my service,
and as not to pass on my syphilis
I'd fuck my wife with a strap-on dildo:
she tells me she's pregnant two weeks ago!"
Mon frère, I didn't know VD'd undone so many . . .

    I handed him a quarter and continued
on my way, headed for the Main; short-cutting
across McGill U. commons' sward, I fell in
with a small group of grad students, legs criss-
crossed like their chirognomic arguments.
They chased Tampico bombers the size of telescopes
with double shots of *Cazadores*.
Under the moon, through a cannabin lens,
they extemporized on everything under everything
under the moon under the idea of the moon,
from the metaphysics of ontology to the ontology of metaphysics,
suffixing "-ness" to their terms

(i.e. *thingness*, *beingness*) so as to effect or affect
— I could not tell the difference —
the gravitasness of their philosophiness,
making a chiasmic messness of my mindness.
Bomber after bomber after bomber,
double shot after shot after shot.
It proved, for me, too much and not enough.
Amidst the "quote-unquote" of it all, I
picked up and moved on, totally bombed.
I stopped in an alley off Milton Street
to wizz; spiced with the finest black pepper,
my *añejo* piss steamed up into my sinuses, clearing
the congested jesting of sound-imagery,
syndactylic phonophanopoiesis —
of Lord Minimus boffing Minnie Mouse;
Daffy Fuck as Apollo, ducking Daphne;
Eeyore Winters lecturing to Pooh on the history
of American Obscurantism; House of Prada
Pratītyasamutpāda; Echo blowing Umberto Eco
while wearing a pair of sneakers by Mark Eckō;
sprezzatura sopressata sandwiches;
Fred Flynt-stone directing gonzo starring
best friends Betty, Wilma, and a brontosaurus-bone
dildo; dinosaurs covering Dinosaur Jr.'s 1994
hit-single "Feel the Pain" (with big-bang irony);
a parmesan-cheese rendering of Parma-
gianino's *Self-Portrait in a Convex Mirror*;
Il Sodoma's *120 Days of Sodom* altarpiece;
Benjy Compson in Compton (L.A.), sitting
on a stoop with Doughboy and Dooky
contemplating the otherness of Time, signifyin'
nothing — in my fried blitzkrieged mind
(would you, dear Reader, as I proceed upon

traveling this exterior interiority, be more inclined
to make sumthin' of nuthin' if my surname
concluded with that diacritical mark which signifies
fortune-cookie wisdom: Porcō?
Wild rough seas tonight: / Snowy galaxies).

    INTERMEZZO. From the *symbolic* rabbit-ear
rabble-"rubble" *nel mezzo del cammin* between my ears,
a literal littoral ozone-smoke proceeded
to unfold enfold an *imaginary* alley *real* rabbit hole.
Muggled cartoon dreamscapes gave way to Dutch angles
shot with wide lenses; the situation, here:
tense (present); neo-neo-neo-real; snapping
Venetian blinds, up-down, don't help matters;
shadows shadowed shadows shadowing
shadowing shadowed shadows shadows;
put your hands where I can seem 'em;
liars, cheaters, grifters; brass-knuckled muscle;
bean-shooter cowards, on the nut hoodlums;
flophouse louses; nose-candy dandies, lazy Daisies;
hammers and saws blurring the law, bustin'
acromegalic jaws on stutterin' spider pricks; di-
ectic Private Dicks; Nevada gassin' rascals; gat-
gammed molls, their complex complexions,
mirrors mirroring mirrored mirrors mirroring
mirrored mirrors, their kisses filling me
with existential bliss and intentional phalluses
and Freudian fallacies and, and, and, and
Christ, what a crisis! So modern, so hip;
it's late, and I'm alienated, a *stranger*
givin' testimony, headed for the wooden kimono.
Oh, no. *Dial H for "Help!"* Operator, save me
(what's yer rate?) from *The* (metaphoric) *Big Sleep*.
The ozone-smoke closin' in, like a

Force of Evil or a storm on *Key Largo*,
it whisks me up, and, like that, I'm (dime)
dropped, *The Wrong Man*, *Breathless*, into
a crowd of tube-topped *Gildas* and *Lauras*,
at the corner of St. Laurent and Prince Arthur. Sober-
ish. *Tout de Suite*. INTERMEZZO FINIS.
    To *The Copa*, at St. Laurent and Bagg.
The city's Anglo-literati (*sans* Lola, Tony, or Rico)
philosophized amid the plastic palm-tree deco,
defending aesthetic *poops du jour*, everything from
Transcendental-Lentil (which Whitman ate
from Emerson's plate) to Bourou-
Bourou Dada ("house special" at the *Cabaret
Voltaire*); from Split Pea *Stil Novisti*
to Beat-Beet (i.e. Borscht); from Olson
Minestrone to Basho-flavoured Fufu Haiku;
from Cock-a-Leekie 'Pataphyseekie to
the Meat Queens (Plath, Sexton) of Confessional *Chil-
li Con Carne*; from OuLiPo Porridge to
Countie Cullen-Slink and, lest we forget,
Wole Soyinka's Solyanka, "favourite"
of all present bleeding-heart liberal diners.
(Pasolini's *Salo*'s a coprologist's light appetizer
compared to such a galimatias pageant of shit.)
A portly Professor, Ph.D., Stanford, sat alone,
ignored, in this darkest recess of Word and world;
he apologized on the antiquated Art
of *Poiesis*, a "moral mode" of being,
a "technique of contemplation," a rational composition
that, like and with Philosophy or Religion,
is the necessary accompaniment to
an everyday living of the highest order.
"*Ready writing makes not good writing,*

and ready living makes not good living.
The capital of -isms determines the form of your *frisson*:
Children, everyday is opposite day;
the opposite of knowing is play without play.
If you never think, you never have a thought;
cogito ergo sum ergo you *are* are not.
Words are yours, and there is a choice to be made:
Moderation enables Liberty, Freedom, and Will;
Rhyme, metre, and diction are the pure thrill
of fidelity to my lovely, lovely wife of thirteen years.
Miss, would you . . . yes, please, another beer."
Of course, nobody listened, his words lost
in the labyrinthine tropical foliage,
a solitary voice dying dying dying in the noise of Carthage.
And me, I tripped balls in the *ion* john
to move this picaresque tale along to its pen-
ultimate finale [DRAMATIC PAUSE]. Action:
I blew through the swinging doors chewing cheroot
between my teeth and looking mean;
from out of its zip, my unholstered schlong drawn
with the heroic elasticity of Plastic Man
(my homage to Montreal's Leonard Cohen)
shot across the room, pissing in shitee-soups,
one by one, when at last *oui-oui* my
ding-dong did settle in a seat at the table
of sad M. Hiver for a last nightcap.
Let Death's blow be executed with mannered
formality — even Michael Corleone
enjoyed the veal before whacking Captain McClusky.
My comic-western dick coiled around
Hiver's neck, choking out one last breath
as soft as a punning snowflake:
"Self-Pity is unbecoming of a poem, even more so of a Man.

So long, farewell, ta-ta, adieu, EXEUNT."

On I ventured toward that place
("Why the mystery, Augustine?") of enough
"poetic" pedigree that these peripatetic thoughts
should at least seem to you not to be tiny-
tots without sure footing ("Whatever is going to happen
is already") but rather fully stepped
in *syzygy*, as I ascend the boulevard's not-so-steep
steep of mock-epic shtick, lickety-split.
Hail Muse, like a taxi, and so on, and so forth,
as my verse proceeds to its converse,
O o o bless me father for I —
to the Church of the *Madonna della Difesa*.
The cupola-moon projected impressionist
light onto the garden façade: red brick billowed
like a sloop's sail. The St. Lawrence wind,
as willed as a snail, cooled my craquelure forehead —
but not enough. I was cracking up; I was dead!
I stowed away aboard "The Rialto." What follows
(via voice-over narration) is just what *I* saw:
"On the river Jordan our sloop moved s l o w l y;
I sat on the bow, staring down intently
at the water that, at times, was more mud
than lickwud. Thick, textured, slip-slop yuk. I sensed,
with the fullness of a midday sun and
by a slight adjustment of my perspective that,
like looking at an anamorphic rebus by Erhard Schön,
say, his *Hinaus, du alter Tor!*, I should un-
conceal the meaning of its text, 'seeking wildly to escape
my fate,' a *pathetic fallacy of a violent mind*.
And, in fact, that's just what happened;
the river's stillness flooded with moving stills:
of Jesus' baptism, which 'didst sanctify the element

of water to the mystical washing away of sin';
of that Syrian General, Naaman, who,
swimming seven times in the river, cured his
syphilitic soul; of the Roman harlot, Chloe, to whom
clitoral tissue was restored
after a skinny-dip, as was her feeling for
the feeling of *Love*'s deep-dick;
of 'Geffrey Chaucer,' who inked in the Jordan
that quill which scribbled his retraction,
Heere taketh the makere of this book his leve;
of Thomas Lodge, who, in the 'Preface'
to his *Prosopopeia* (1596), asked
to be 'cleansed, from the leprosy of my
lewd lines, in the Jordan of Grace';
of Dr. Donne who said young Jack was a quack
who didn't know the first thing about Love
'til he kissed the mouth of the Jordan;
of John Wilmot, libertine, esquire, his dis-
sembled powder-face, when splashed
with *nahr al-urdun*, collapsed into a rainbow
that floated downstream and with it
taking Rochester's memory of every erotic dream;
and a final image, or rather half-image
(a cold shadow forced the sun to shiver away
before I could figure the total frequency
of the form) of he who I believed to be Porco
(Alessandro), the pornographic poet
('Why him?' I made out his pierced tragus,
and the tattoo of Kelly, Jill, on his neck),
sitting with his back to the bank; and if
he laughed or cried I could not tell the difference
by his convulsions. The meaning was lost.
He sat, alone, waiting without hope, for more and less than the sun."

Hieronymus Tugnutt in Love

I

In Boschland
did Tugnutt knock nock,
and in hogeye bacchi
winkel and wame
the quimwig quimbush;
fuzzymuzzy yawns
of the city, world-wary —
too, too much so
to ginch, zither or futz
with any impression of dee-
light: jutsum just some,
I would weary, bid
thingamy, and good-blite!

II

On a polly-nussy
summer's day, chuftie enough
to make a kipper twitchet
like titmouse on baz,
there's no place more muffet
to Tugnutt's eyes
— children scat about
afternoonies
amusing themselves with
games of Snutchies —
the tweens wexperiwent wixing
conchita and whidgey,
only to wind up diddlypout
above the toilet
wubbling to God —
and the folks
gig hefty-clefty on the Tenuc
shore, or some-
some the timetime jody
on porches like pip-
kin, while their jibs jib.

III

Down
whelk zouzoune,
the *Musée des Poontenanny*
schmoya of Goya fl-
unked by
gammon of Lautreamont and
Matisse mapatasi,
twat blivvets — the likes
of which dollup for cooch rides
whipped by gimcracks
oosy-doosy
Yum-yum, Pum-pum,
Spadger, and Stinkpot streets.

IV

Come dark, the Moon —
yellow,
with abstract
muliebral of monilia —
to quote from
Pintle de Case (Boschland's
anaphoric Poet Laureate),
is

> *poe tootsie-wootsie*
> *poe hoecake hawsehole*
> *poe dumbsquint cunnikin*

And goosed beyond dingle
(alas, when in do, do
as they do, or risk the calamity
of a glamity tag such as
gewgaw tosser or *poof todger*,
nonny-nonny shaken oaf
with cerassie ease)
every Tugnutt straps his futz
taut as his Achilles
and hiles the holla-
waymile up the skirts of Boschland
where Madam Colpyle's
pleidid daughters
— loquacious Loquens,
Jaxy and Joxy, her -xious twins,
moot Moot, and la tou-
louse Sluice —
twirly-whirly his ding-ding . . .

V

"O swallow, why wench
ile bliff you," Hieronymous
Tugnutt's in love —

Just Passing Through

Taste so good, make a grown man cry, sweet cheery pie.
— Warrant

I came upon the road sign, TRY OUR SWEET CHERRY PIE,
and thought, why not? "Miss, one piece, please, of cherry pie."

Cherry — that's what her name-tag said, in red, I swear
— served my order, her local smile as warm as cherry pie.

Cherries dotted the diner's white walls. The décor recalled
the bedsheets that night I first had at *mon* virgin *chéri's* pie.

Two salesmen to my left chit-chatted about vacuum bits;
I wanted badly to stuff their pieholes shut with cherry pie.

I bowed to say Grace. Cherry steam condensed on my
piously bent face. "Thank you, O Lord, for cherry pie."

Upon that first delicious bite, bitter cherry-sized tears fell
from my eyes — I had no love with whom to share my pie!

There was a wino, his stink carrying like a cirrhotic sirocco.
So much so, twice I thought my cherry pie a Sherry pie.

Done. Yum. My dish licked clean, white as *sakura* blossoms
in spring — surely even ascetic Bashō indulged in cherry pie.

Epigram: On Postmodernity

Jass,
clazzical.

Bob Alan Deal

I – *The Grapes of Susan*

Squeezed like a Fender fret-board — mom, dad,
Baby Susan — we packed the '59 Ford and drove
Across country, an Exodus to Garden Grove (CA).
I was five. The Surfaris, The Ventures, Dick Dale —
Surf-rock ruled the air- and ocean-waves, its loud
Tremolo ro-rolling like the tide; orange trees
Lined city streets, conduit fruits for surf-sound
Reverb squeezed-out like rhino-chasers to Hawaii.
The weather was just about perfect for "Bird" —
Our pet name for Susan — whose young lung
Collapsed at birth — that's why we said so long
To Huntington (IN), as per the Doctor's order:
     The arid climate, he said, would help her survive;
     As for me, I strapped on a guitar for dear life.

II – *Bad Is How I Was Born: Bob Alan Deal*

Pop some Seconal, chase it with a Sloe Gin,
Or Bellar — the drink I concocted to get cocked —
One part Kahlua, one part brandy, all rock;
Snort an ant, bum a tab of mescaline —
Be somebody. Back in high school, Mr. Hickock
Asked his students to write a short paper on
A favourite poem — Frost and Emerson
Had nothing on "Pressed Rat and Warthog"
(Cream), so I skipped class, I flipped-off school.
Chase the dream: sex, drugs, booze. *Be cool.*
Hop the magic carpet, ride the La-la high to the stars;
Be somebody, Bob Alan Deal. Be Mick Mars:
    I play lead — riffs and licks — for *Mötley Crüe*;
    I was born B.A.D., but it's a pleasure to meet you.

III – *The Midnight Gardener of the Santa Monica Mountains*

A cannibal, a King — of Borneo, and in love
With a serf — and, a serf myself, too — previous
Incarnations — Wahtoshi — White Horse —
The Stone Pony — and Ziggy Charlemagne —
Each of me connected like a Vivid-girl daisy chain.
For a time I rented a cozy three-bedroom
Pad, as close to the moon and stars as
One could ever imagine; and a hobo-shaman,
The Midnight Gardener, he tended my lawn,
My flower beds, plucking the weeds, trimming
Stems. *We are each descendant from*
Someone, or something else, he believed:

    A King, a beggar, a greater, a lesser being;
    And we tripped out on chi till morning.

IV — . . . *And all through the house*

'Tis the season to be, and the Christmas tree
Vince, Tommy, and St. Nikki pinched from a lot,
With the help of — I think — Hans Naughty,
Was decorated in beer, needles 'n' snot —
The thin pine branches carried more disease
Than scraps of North Hollywood ass crashed
On our kitchen floor; trash piled on trash.
Neighbours filed official complaints with the city
For the stink; the landlord reported a rank-
Stank tub brimming with used tampons and pads;
Roaches rimmed the sink, nibbling at scabs —
And at each other, hopped-up on vermin smack.
    I kept mine clean — my livelihood, my hands —
    Clean as one can when you're "with the band."

V – *Shout at the Devil*

After losing his baby girl, Skylar, to a tumor,
Vince kicked sobriety and checked into a stupor;
Tommy served time in the can for the smack
He laid on a pregnant Pam; medics officially "called"
Nikki — only he walked up to the light, said Hi
To Jesus, saw the sights, and walked right on back;
Zoloft and Wellbutrin, my two favourite aliens,
Phosphorescent orange, abducted my head,
While *Ankylosing Spondylitis* — degenerative — had
Everything else — my spine, joints, ligaments, and limbs:
The slightest move set off the launch code,
And I braced for the shooting pains to explode.
    Crushed like Zombie Dust, corked in a vial:
    The higher we rock, the harder we fall.

Two Flowers: After Giuseppe Ungaretti

one inexpressible two

Poem
(The *AVN* Remix)

A translation of Stephen Cain's translation of Frank O'Hara's
"Khrushchev is coming on the right day!"

Peter North is coming on the right Avy Scott!
                              the cool graced Nikita
is pushed off the enormous Lex Steele by hard Gina Ryder
and everything is tossing, hurrying on up
                              this Tabitha Stevens
has everything but *politesse*, a Sydnee Steele Monica Mayhem says
and five different Chloe I see
                    look like reptile cages
with her blonde Brianna Banks tossing, too,
                              as she looked when I pushed
her little Devon on the Hannah Harper on the Jezebelle Bond it
                              was also windy

last Flick Shagwell we went to an Alana Evans and came out,
                              Eva Angelina
                              is greater
than armchair, silicon said, that's what I think, blueberry Dru
                              Barrymore
and zipper was probably being carped at
                    in Ashley Blue, no *politesse*
silicon tells me about his Sylvia Saint trip to Tyler Faith
                              bottle tells us
about his Summer Cumming's life in Pavlina Valentova, it sounds
                              like Rocco's
painting *Tera Patrick*
              so I go Nina Hartley to Ginger Lynn and Rachel Rotten
                    drift through my Kinzie Kenner

plane ticket, pool table and cuttlefish,
    all
        unknown Shayla Laveaux of the early Jenna Haze as I go
                          to Olivia O'Lovely

where does the Cal Jammer of the Shelbee Myne go
                     when Stacy Valentine
                     takes Bridgette Kerkove
and turns it into ozone Aria Giovanni
                Amber of Lynns
                so I get back up
make Ashlyn Gere, and read tea leaves, her Victoria Givens so dark
    Tiffany Million seems blinding and my Asia Carrera is
                    blowing up the Bunny Luv
I wish I would blow off
            though it is cold and somewhat warms my Calli Cox
as the Holly Sampson bears zipper on to Inari Vachs
    and the Alexis Amore seems to be eternal
    and Jenna Jameson seems to be inexorable
    I am foolish enough always to find it in Jill Kelly

If They've Compared You . . .

for Brenna

If they've compared you to a delightful romantic comedy from
    Germany
If they've compared you to Eugenio Montale's "If they've compared
    you . . ."
If they've compared you to a sugar-lipped glass of *Campari*, as
    if to say, "Baby, you're so bittersweet," a paradox that may
    (fingers crossed) or may not (fingers crossed) destroy the
    world
If they've compared you to the carnal-red cardinal that comes and
    goes, comes and goes, outside your constantly inconstant window

If they've compared you to flora — orchis and gentian, fern and whip
    -scirpus, mushroom and sponge, hypnum and hydnum —
    before the fawning imperative of "Let's make love"
If they've compared you to upstate New York, especially Schenectady
    and Metonym
If they've compared you or, more specifically, your breasts, to the
    umlaut
If they've compared you to music, be deaf to it

If they've compared you to a spy, you are truly Elizabethan, at least
    in conceit
If they've compared you to a *chemise à la reine*, will you suffer a fate
    like that of Marie Antoinette?
If they've compared you to a rather long line of verse, thus implicitly
    expressing reservations with regard to your sense of propriety,
    sexual or otherwise
If they've compared you . . . and by "they" I mean "I"

It's because you both are and are not imaginary and not-imaginary
It's because both they and I are lost and alone, that is, unconditionally
   conditional

She's All That

I gather my thoughts
And tally my loss:
As thin-spun as eidyllia
And Cavalli as a dahlia;
As saucy as a calzone,
More fatale than a Hanzo;
As golden as a waffle,
And airy as a wiffleball;
As posterior as Beyoncé,
And dicey as Yahtzee;
As nuts as Arabian Goggles,
And impotent as Gogol;
As pure as pure ya-yo,
And Bronx as Jenny J-Lo;
As deep fried as a Twinkie,
More spring than a Slinky;
As drunk as Tara Reid,
And pastoral as a reed;
As Vivid as Jenna J.,
And weialala as the Thames;
As artificial as Miss June,
Deeper than an Orient moon,
As wickedawesome as the Red Sox,
And big-haired as cock rock;
As limber as a stripper,
And stellar as the Big Dipper;
As seedy as anise,
Less lezzy than Lisa Leslie;
As caramel as a macchiato,
And accultured as arigato;

As pumped as a keg,
And kicked as a Rockette;
As huzzah as Keats,
And facial as skeet;
As twenty-sixed as abecedarius,
More schizo than Cerberus;
As ruff-ruff as woof-woof,
Less muff than Naomi Wolf;
As kiminoed as a geisha,
And A.B.C. as Iesha;
As cluck-cluck as a chickenhead ho,
And, like Mya, "an ass like . . . *whoa*!"
As death-dealing as Selene,
And dreamy as neoprene;
As glittery as the gulch,
And nonce as a ginch;
Anything but effete,
She's as fit as a rhymed couplet;
As deep-dicked as an ovary,
And avoutrious as Madame Bovary;
As cool-minty as a mojito,
And wet as mojado;
As emancipated as Mimi,
And Mami to my Papi;
As fresh as a bidet,
And poison, po-po-poison, as B.B.D.
("That girl is . . .")
A squirter like Avy Scott,
As lucky as a bank shot,
As boo-yah as Stuart Scott,
C.R.E.A.M. as the money shot —
Cash rules everything around me!
The *objet petit a* of all my love and dap:

As dry as a sand-trap
Is my most Mango-Genie-Tini
With a bod like Barbara Eden!
Sweet Laura to my Luke,
As confederate as Daisy Duke;
As Samoan as a fog-cutter,
Cutting through catarrh;
As allacabam as tooraloorals,
And crowned by laurels;
As cha-ching as a slot machine,
More Duff than a teen queen;
As rub as a dub-dub,
And rhizomed as rhubarb;
As blupa as tequila,
And fishscale as kilos;
As delumnimate as Hesiod,
And blue-eyed as woad;
As mad-libbed as smiddys,
And jibbed as ditties;
More divine than chimera,
And clit-hopped as Asia Carrera;
As strophed as Stroh's,
And fly as a farfallo;
As prosecutorial as Kincaid,
And krunk as kinkav;
A gushing winged lover
As pluvial as a plover;
As luxuriate as lussorioso,
And lush as a rostro;
As warm as a winter's Saki,
And Porco as Miyazaki;
More mondo than a demimonde,
And gooooooooooooooooooal as Telemundo;

As brewski as a brouhaha,
And fugee as fugeelala —
That's the way that she rocks
doing her thang!
As tight-boxed as a hookah,
More flower-fingered than ochra;
More stuffed than gooducken,
And Hooterville as Petticoat Junction;
Like Leibniz's monad,
Or a Dionysian maenad;
Like King Kong's Dwan,
Or Baudelaire's swan;
Like Faust's Gretchen,
Or Nashville's Gretchen;
Like Dante's Beatrice,
Or Kafka's Felice;
Like Montale's Dora Markus,
With a rumba's maracas;
As compound as a kenning,
And loving as Summer Cummings;
As elixic as arcana,
And pura as Purakaunui;
As "open, sesame" as Ali Baba,
The bing to my bada;
As crazed as Castel Pulci,
And hooch as coochie;
As polyphonous as mottetti,
And Polyanna as confetti;
As falutent as Ausonia,
And bethonged as Red Sonja;
As plucked as a plectrum,
And punched as rum;
My sweet sassy *mmmm*-molassee,

And curvacious as massé;
As à la carte as Time,
And tra-la-la as rhyme;
As Petrarchan as a ship's luff,
And, thus, as luff as love;
More Rimbaud than rimjob,
And spring as an Ojo;
As lymphatic as a Limax,
And stut-tut-tutter as a c-c-c-climax;
As gobbed as a knob-shine,
And boned as Stacey Valentine;
As fuoco as Kaley Cuoco,
And moist as a sirocco;
As tough as a goal-line stand,
And tender as a lap-dance;
As lips as Janice Dickinson,
And — um, why not? — Mason to my Dixon;
As seiche as a sashay,
And loyal as Lassie;
As lush as Tara Patrick,
And faithful as [sic];
As libidinal as Fourquet,
And bona fide as a fugazi;
As well-to-do as la-di-das,
And timbaled as cicadas;
Sparkling like a glass of Asti,
And sweet as *stilnovisti*;
Zippin like Pippin,
Like a riptide rollride of riddim,
And the same as the same as the same as the idem;
As slipped as sipple,
And sipple as syllables;
As gay as Laetitia,

And polychromatic as Titian;
Jelly-rolled like a zigzag,
More ziggedy than gadzooks;
As tagged as wildstyle,
And loving as a philophile;
As larval as a polliwog
Smoking pole like a polewig;
As perilous as Pauline,
And plebeian as a plene spleen;
As yum as a cumswap,
More bounce than a Dunlop;
As prostrate as Philostrate,
And lost as the Bering Strait;
More O.C. than Chino,
Ergo as capuchin as cappucino;
As architextual as Chinampas,
As magnetic as a compass,
Though flatter than La Pampas;
My sweet Fregoli delusion,
Who despises all things Deleuzian!
As Cinci as a bowtie,
And freaky-deaky as hentai;
Blazoned like a mistress,
And *festschrift* as all of this —
Or as *as* as *as*
And more *more* than *more*. . .
She's all that — 'n' a bag of chips;
And sure as dill's pickled, she's sure gone.
And Don Tugnutt, he's all alone,
An ass as assless as assless chaps.

Chuck Neiderman's "To His Coy Mistress"
(The *Necessary Roughness* Remix)

Time timalaya timalina timarooskie
Coy coyalaya coyalina coyarooskie
Lady ladylaya ladylina ladyrooskie
Veggie veggilaya veggilina veggirooskie
Love lovalaya lovalina lovarooskie
Grow growalaya growalina growarooskie
Vast vastalaya vastalina vastarooskie
Slow slowalaya slowalina slowarooskie
Thy thyalaya thyalina thyarooskie
Heart heartalaya heartalina heartarooskie
    Winged wingalaya wingalina wingarooskie
Hurry hurrylaya hurrylina hurryrooskie
Song songalaya songalina songarooskie
Dust dustalaya dustalina dustarooskie
Lust lustalaya lustalina lustarooskie
Grave gravalaya gravalina gravarooskie
    Now nowalaya nowalina nowarooskie
Youth youthfulaya youthfulina youthfulrooskie
Roll rollalaya rollalina rollarooskie
Ball ballalaya ballalina ballarooskie
Life lifalaya lifalina lifarooskie
Sun sunalaya sunalina sunarooskie
Stand standalaya standalina standarooskie
Run runalaya runalina runarooskie

The Minutes

For every minute is expectancy
Of more arrivance.

— Shakespeare

Let's begin: graduate students
in Poetics at SUNY Buffalo
give awful blowjobs; they've
no sense of rhythm
these ladies (please read
Derek Attridge's *The Rhythms*
of English Poetry).
There is always a case
to be made. The most misused
word in the language is
sublime (adolescent sublime;
capitalist sublime; urban
sublime; Pittsburgh Steelers
sublime; Brazilian wax
sublime; sublime sublime).
The trouble with sincerity
is the trouble with everything.
The Lord our Saviour is
a mediocre sonneteer at best,
as any formal study of
Jones Very's *Collected Poems*
makes clear. I have nothing
to add; I have nothing to add
to "I have nothing to add."
Everyone always thinks
he is the exception to
the rule; but not I. In this, *I*

am the exception to the
rule. [Insert your hip anti-
war slogan here.] Quote. Hey,
go fuck yourself. Unquote.
#37 on my list of 100 things
I could do without: poems
about getting your first period.
New evidence suggests that
Saint Augustine toyed with
the idea of titling Book Three
of his *Confessions*
"What happens in Carthage
stays in Carthage."
On this day in history
the stars were shining bright
on somebody. Meeting adjourned.

*

Let's begin: satisfy your
maternal urge, adopt
a highway. I am a knot
in desperate need of *deus
ex machina* but this
ain't your daddy's Horace.
The word of the day is
not "ontology" (Nov. 20th). Jazz
hands. I saw mommy
kissing Santa Claus but
it wasn't on the mouth. Jazz
hands. #49 on my list
of 100 "must-read" books
of scholarship written by

certified Counts is Korzybski's
Introduction to Non-
Aristotelian Systems &
General Semantics.
Schlupp, schlupp, schlupp.
"Your lips look so
delicious upon a tropical shore
before blizzard season."
I'm very attracted to you.
Everyone misunderstands
a lyric. Like tulips in a pond.
On this day in history
the Anglo -licious (from
the Latin *licia*) is suffixed to
STD-related terms so as
to put a positive spin
on an otherwise bad situation:
herpelicious, siphylicious,
papillomalicious, clapalicious.
I'm seeing stars.
Meeting adjourned.

*

Let's begin: shalom, whilom.
Do you read me? Copy.
Do you read me? Copy.
The stars are out early tonight.
#69 on my list of 100
ways to make poetry more
popular with "the kids": rename
the Gerald Lampert Award (GLA)
the Ginger Lynn Award (GLA),

to be given annually in recognition
of the poetess with the
best-looking cooch in Canada.
Is this thing on? Quote. Go
take a flying Philadelphia fuck
in a rolling doughnut. Un-
quote. LOL. Only in the movies
is the piranha a monster.
*69. Satire requires traction.
Japanese travelogues by
young idealistic Westerners
focus exclusively on the
"lyric intensity" of haiku or
the "spiritual intensity" of Eastern
philosophy or the "sublime
intensity" of Rashomon Gate
but (cf. yo' mama) fail to mention
time and money spent in
Yokohama sex shops, home
of the chin dildo. Join
the revolution for only $19.99;
some assembly required.
You say *tomato*, I say *to-mah-to*;
You say *potato*, I say *po-tah-to*;
You say *ethics*, I say *cum-dump-ster*.
Let's call the whole thing off.
Meeting adjourned.

Mottetti

Hello.
Telos.

*

This is the saddest story.
We took the stairs to a happier one.

*

Once upon a time.
Once upon a time.

*

Mote.
Emote.

*

She invited me upstairs for coffee.
Res not *verba*.

*

Omit.
Obit.

*

It was a day like any other.
Other.

*

Misp
laced.

*

Little.
A little later.

*

Empyreal,
Empirical.

*

I am
things in things.

*

She loves me *and* he loves me.
A love-me knot.

*

Still
still.

*

Language.
Gag.

And Your Nightgown Is White:
After Salvatore Quasimodo

And you stare me down;
and your nightgown
is white, and one white breast
— your left — exposed.

And the white moon's
white light lightly strokes
your shoulders; it exceeds me.

Words, words, words
that once worked
to hearten this existence
have since deserted Life's circus.

Yet what is the wind
that descends upon our bed
certain nights of March —

a wind that has me turn
to you, and return
to you, as if for the first time?

Atechnical Synthetic Futurist Theatre for Nine Voices, for Performance on MTV (The *Laguna Beach* Remix)

INSTRUCTIONS FOR PERFORMANCE

The piece consists of nine sections, each notated on a separate index card. An identical pile of the nine cards is presented to each performer.

Performances are simultaneous. The order in which the cards are performed is entirely at the discretion of each individual (shuffle, if necessary, for variety).

All cards must be used at least once.

Avoid moments of uniform silence amongst the nine performers.

Duration is indeterminate but should not exceed nine minutes. For best results, select overly effusive gay men; or, the most sexually attractive female poets below the age of thirty in Canada; or Coach House Books poets.

*

1 - WHAT-everrrrrr WHAT-everrrrrrr WHAT-everrrrrrr

2 - that's super soooo super that's super soooo super

3 - uh-huh totally uh-huh totally uh-huh totally uh-huh totally

4 - ohmygod ohmygod ohmygod ohmygod ohmygod

5 - like do you like him or do you like like like him?

6 - fersure fersure fersure fersure fersure fersure fersure

7 - anywayz anywayz anywayz anywayz anywayz anywayz

8 - knowwhatImean? knowwhatImean? knowwhatImean?

9 - 'kay 'kay 'kay 'kay 'kay 'kay 'kay 'kay 'kay 'kay

Keg Stand: After Jean-Baptiste Chassignet (1594)

Think how below your fieldstone the earthworms
    embalm your body like some B-movie
    flesh-eating disease; and how your bones de-
materialize, turn to shit, they fertilize the very dirt you're in.

See your right hand, which once felt-up girls' skirts,
    it rots, disowned, feels nothing; your eyeballs slinky
    from their sockets. The earthworms mosey
on over to your musculature like cows to pasture.

In case you're wondering, *your* drawn belly's bilious
    stink's got neighbouring dead running from their caskets;
        your de-faced nose face-fucks your cheekbone.

Look, I ain't asking you be a snob connoisseur of human
    finitude; to take stock, as if Life's a fine wine,
        only wastes Time — stand on your head, tap Love's keg.

We So Seldom Look on Nantucket (I - XXI)

I – *Ancient Egypt, Home of the Limerick*

"There was once a Goddess named Isis,
Blinded by spunk in her eyesis:
    Her eyeballs inflamed,
    Ra's balls were to blame —
Creation myth or conjunctivitis?"

II – *Get Bent, Baby*

"I once met the Whore of Krakow,
Who, blessed with a bent for kowtow,
    Would get on her knees
    And eat her own pussy;
An agile gal, that crazy Whore of Krakow."

III – *The Whore of Mont Royal*

"I once met a Whore on Mont Royal,
Who lathered my junk in sex oils;
    A botanical extract
    Soothed my chafed shaft
And cooled the itch of my cock boils."

IV – *Harold Bloom and the Gypsy Whore*

"There once was a Gypsy Whore,
Who vagibonked from door to door;
    Wholly transhumptive
    — *Thou Art what They give* —
Metaleptic gypsic [sic] whore."

V – *Psalm 137* (after Jenna Jameson)

"By the Rivers of Babylon,
My captors demanded a song —
    But why would I sing?
    I spread my ding-ding,
Instead, for their dirty foreign schlongs."

VI – *The Bolivian Ztink*

"There once was a Whore in La Paz,
Who asked, 'You like do blow my azz?'
    Before I could decline,
    She had fixed me a line.
With my nose on her azz she pazzed la gaz."

VII – *The Whore of Dundee*

"I once met the Whore of Dundee,
Who promptly slipped off her undies;
      She spread her 'auld lang'
      (That's Scots for 'poontang')
And I tapped dat wee lassie indeedee."

VIII – *Oh so Pre-Post-Para-Avant!*

"There fümms was a bö wö from Rinnzekete,
Who Rrummpff his cash in a rakete;
      But his grimm, named Glimm,
      Ran gnimm with bimbimm,
And bö wö the rakete, Rinnzekete."

IX – *St. Bernadette's All Wet*

"I once had a vision at Lourdes
— Not of Mary, but of Traci Lords;
      It fits that Jesus
      Rimes with 'O, Jesus!'
Cuz I saw Traci blowing the Lord."

X – *Support the Troops*

"I gleefully humped Paula Abdul
During a U.S.O. tour-stop at Kabul —
    A barrack commandeered
    She proceeded to steer
My cold-hearted snake to her alalae-abdul."

XI – *All that Matters is Alma Mater*

"There once was a Whore of Corvallis:
A State U. Beaver named Alice;
    She refused to fuck
    Oregon Ducks,
That principled Whore of Corvallis."

XII – *Why I Write Limericks* (after Barbara Gowdy)

"I met an old Whore on Nantucket:
As we humped she kicked the bucket;
    But I stayed the course
    And spunked in her corpse:
We so seldom look on Nantucket!"

XIII – *Seize the Snatch*

"There once was a pornstar from Lima,
Who didn't mind swallowing semen —
    But Miss Alexis Amore
    Thought BJs a bore
And would much rather *carpe* munch *diem*."

XIV – *Tits, Tats, and the Other Thing*

"There once was a broad named Mitzy,
She had a jubnormous pair of titzies —
    But chronic pimples
    On each of her nipples
Kept Mitzy's titzies from my lipzies."

XV – *A Knight's Tale*

"There once was a Princess amputee,
Arms to her elbows, legs to her knees;
    Just a head and a stump
    'Twas my duty to hump;
She: 'My thanks, kind Knight, for your perversity.'"

XVI – *Open for Jizzness*

"There once was a Whore at Nantucket,
2010's "Miss Cum Bucket,"
    Opening her throat
    For white-hot loads
From tourists tired of tugnutting it."

XVII – *Reading Jenna J. into Kant's* Second Critique

"Kant philosophized a *summum bonum*,
As if anticipating Jenna J.'s bum
    — Her highest goody
    So inspires my woody
With but two swift tugtugs I cumcum."

XVIII – The Canzoniere *as Limerick*

"There was once a gal named Laura,
Who flashed 'round town like a Whora;
    Not a day did pass
    Without her Avignon ass
Causin' Frankie to cry, 'Oh Laura.'"

XIX – *Product*

"There once was a gal named Erica,
Who got totally freakin' hysterica
    When Tugnutt withdrew
    And said, 'How d'you do?'
With North-like loads to her hairica."

XX – *The Limerick as Ontological Nightmare*

". . . There was once there once was once there was
Once was there was there once was once there
    There was once there once was
    Once there was once was there
Was there once was once there there was once . . ."

XXI – *Poetry Makes Nothing Happen*

"There once was a Whore of Parnassus,
With an inspiring poetic assus:
    Don Tugnutt's love-juice
    Flooded his Muse —
A Castalian spring sprang from her assus."

Acknowledgements

My thanks to Jason Camlot, David McGimpsey, and Carolyn Smart; to my editor Michael Holmes and ECW Press; and to my always loving and supportive Porco family.

For much of the local detail in "Bob Alan Deal," I am indebted to that poem's source text, Mötley Crüe's *The Dirt: Confessions of the World's Most Notorious Rock Band*. The instructive performance notes for "Atechnical Synthetic Futurist Theatre for Nine Voices . . ." are borrowed, in part, from Steve McCaffery's Dilemma of the Meno" (*Seven Pages Missing*).

Eadem Mutata Resurgo